God's Last Altar Call

MARK FINLEY
with STEVEN MOSLEY

Pacific Press Publishing Association
Boise, Idaho
Oshawa, Ontario, Canada

Edited by B. Russell Holt
Cover art by Nathan Greene
Designed by Judi Paliungas, Center Graphics, Newbury Park, CA
Typeset in 10/12 New Century Schoolbook

Copyright © 1995 by
Pacific Press Publishing Association
Printed in the United States of America
All rights reserved

All Bible quotations are from the New King James Version unless otherwise credited.

ISBN 0-8163-1263-X

Contents

Before You Turn This Page 5

The Pocket-Sized God 7

A Tale of Two Churches 19

When Shepherds Turn Into Beasts 29

Can It Reach the Whole World? 41

Before You Turn This Page

The party of Arctic explorers was marooned on a rocky, barren island. Shivering, they huddled together. The end was inevitable; they were going to freeze to death. Apparently, there was no hope. Then one of them spotted a puff of smoke on the horizon. That single puff of smoke buoyed their spirits. It was an indication that help was on the way, that deliverance was coming. That puff of smoke was a message of encouragement.

Is there a message of hope for our weary, war-torn world today? Is there a message of encouragement for our confused, chaotic planet? Is help on the way?

There has never been a time in world history during a major crisis affecting God's people that God has not sent a message of warning and encouragement and comfort. In the days of Noah, God planned to destroy this world with a flood. But He sent a man with a warning message to prepare men and women for the crisis. Accepting Noah's message meant life; rejecting Noah's message meant death. Those who accepted the message of salvation and entered the ark were saved. Those who rejected the message were lost. When the world was going to be destroyed by water, God sent that warning message of urgent importance.

Is there a message in our day as important for humanity as Noah's message was for his day? Is there a message from beyond the stars, a message from God Himself, for a generation living at the close of time? Is there a puff of smoke on the horizon for a generation approaching the year 2000? If indeed, we are living in the end time—a time of famine, floods, and earthquakes, a time of rising violence, a time when the sands in the hourglass of time are running out—does God have a special, distinct message for this hour?

Steve Mosley and I are profoundly convinced that He does. We believe the book of Revelation contains God's final message for today. We believe there are specific instructions in the book of Revelation to prepare men and women for the coming crisis that is soon to break on the world.

Come with us. Journey through the pages of the book of Revelation in *God's Last Altar Call*. You will discover God's message for you. You'll discover His final appeal to the human race. This book is not one of many that are written merely to share a few moral principles to live by. This book can be life-changing. It can make a profound difference in your life. It is God's final appeal to you. It is God's last altar call for a race in deep trouble. Come with us prayerfully through these pages and allow God to radically revolutionize and change your life. Discover His insights for today and see your own personal puff of smoke on the horizon.

Mark Finley and Steven Mosley

The Pocket-Sized God

It was Good Friday, April 17, 1987. Debbie Williams and a half dozen friends jumped out of an airplane at 12,000 feet in the clear skies near Phoenix, Arizona. A few seconds into her free-fall, Debbie went into a corkscrew, a fast dive to catch up with four others below her. But she miscalculated her descent and slammed into another diver. The fifty-mile-per-hour impact knocked Debbie unconscious. She bounced away, limp as a rag doll.

Now Debbie was plummeting toward earth, with her parachute unopened—and no way to open it. She hurtled past her instructor and jump master, Gregory Robertson. He noticed blood covering her face. Immediately, Gregory forced his body into a "no-lift" dive—head tucked into his chest, toes pointed, and arms flat at his sides. Quickly he was diving at 180 miles per hour. But when he looked up to check, Debbie still seemed to be falling away from him.

Gregory kept going, trying to dive faster and faster. As the horizon came up to meet him, he maneuvered his shoulders ever so slightly to guide his descent toward the unconscious young woman. And then, he was there beside her, looking for all the world like superman without a cape. Gregory reached out and grabbed Debbie's reserve cord. Yanking it hard, he quickly moved away. Her chute opened, and she began drifting slowly toward the ground.

At two thousand feet, only twelve seconds from impact, Gregory opened his own chute.

Debbie and superman both survived. Debbie would recover fully from her injuries—and remain always grateful to the one who had miraculously snatched her from a fatal impact.

It's my conviction that our world and everyone on it is rushing headlong toward an impact with the end time. We are speeding toward a collision with the final events of earth's history. Wars and rumors of wars, earthquakes, crime, and disease keep rushing at us, telling us that the end is near. And, most important of all, the gospel is going to all the world, sweeping through whole empires where it was shut out before.

If you were God and you knew that the earth was spinning rapidly toward its date with eternity, and that the destiny of millions of people would soon be decided forever, what would your last message of warning be? What would you say—just before the end?

We're plummeting toward ground zero, and a lot of people don't have on a parachute. Even more are simply unconscious; they don't realize that the horizon is rushing up to meet them. But even at this late hour, God has planned a mid-air rescue. Even as we fall headlong, seconds from impact, He has devised a way to help us pull our rip cords.

God's mid-air rescue is described in Revelation, the last book of the Bible. This is what the apostle John saw happening near the close of time:

> Then I saw another angel flying in the midst of heaven, having the everlasting gospel to preach to those who dwell on the earth—to every nation, tribe, tongue, and people (Revelation 14:6).

What a dramatic picture of God attempting to rescue every person on planet Earth! Here is a heavenly messenger "flying in midair" (NIV), flying down to our rescue. He is the first of three angels pictured in Revelation 14 who will issue loud proclamations over the earth. The book of Revelation is full of symbols. These symbolic angels represent God's three final messages. They speak urgent words, and their urgency comes from a caring heavenly Father.

If you look at this chapter carefully, you will see something important. The conclusion of all three messages is found in verse 14, which describes the greatest event in history—the second coming of Jesus, Himself. Here, we see the Son of Man with a golden crown on His head and a sharp sickle in His hand. "The harvest of the earth is ripe," an angel says (verse 15). This is the final judgment, when history reaches its climax and all human destinies are sealed.

Obviously, the three angels' messages that precede Christ's return are vitally important. They are God's final appeal, His last altar call, if you please. In these messages, He is telling us exactly how to open our parachutes as the end of time rushes up to meet us.

In the next three chapters of this little book, we're going to look at these three angels' messages in detail. We will start with the first mid-air message—something that can bring each of us courage and hope. But first, please keep in mind how God's final altar call starts off. It begins with an angel having "the everlasting gospel" to preach. The gospel is the foundation of all three messages. The good news that saved Paul is the same good news that will save the last person living on earth before Jesus comes. There is only one parachute ever made that can rescue sinful human beings—the gospel of Jesus Christ.

So all that these three angels say must be understood

in the context of the true gospel. Forces are unleashed at the end of time that will try to distort and compromise the gospel. That is why God in His mercy and love gives us these warnings. He doesn't want people to panic as the end of time approaches, or to be lulled into sleep. Both panic and lethargy are real dangers as we approach the end. Either will cause us to be unable to grasp the gospel, to pull the rip cord. So let's try to identify this "everlasting gospel" as clearly as we can from the words of Scripture.

When the apostle Paul wanted to define "the gospel which I preached to you," he summed it up in this way:

> I delivered to you first of all that which I also received: that Christ died for our sins according to the Scriptures, and that He was buried, and that He rose again the third day according to the Scriptures (1 Corinthians 15:3, 4).

So the everlasting gospel is first of all this: that Jesus Christ died for our sins. He took in His own body the penalty of human guilt.

Second, at the cross Christ also laid down His perfect life as a substitute for our sinful one. His righteousness is credited to us.

Third, Christ rose from the dead. He came through the ordeal victorious.

Fourth, Christ ascended to the Father and received pardon and acceptance for us on the basis of His sacrifice.

Perhaps these basic facts of the gospel are quite familiar to you. You may think you have heard it all before. But in actuality, powerful forces in our world have been shrinking and distorting the gospel all through history until many of us have lost our ability to really grasp it.

Today, the cross is often reduced to a psychological tool,

a technique for dealing with guilt feelings. "I'm OK; you're OK," is the theme. People tend to shape the gospel in the way that best suits their felt needs.

It's true that the cross deals with human guilt. But Christ's sacrifice solved a problem much bigger than the problem of our human feelings. The "everlasting gospel" is the solution to a specific problem: How can sinful human beings be accepted by a holy God? How can we be pardoned, forgiven, and declared not guilty in the day of judgment? The first five chapters of the book of Romans explain this gospel solution in detail. Justification, what the cross accomplishes, solves the problem of God's righteous judgment.

The most important question facing human beings is this: "What must I do to be saved?" It is the most important question at this moment in your life, and it will be the most important question when you take your last breath. And the cross is the answer to that question. Christ didn't die on the cross just to help us feel better. He sacrificed Himself because of our enormous moral problem. He gave Himself up to the cross in order to rescue us from eternal death. You see, we are sinners—both in nature and in act. And we are responsible before God for our condition and our behavior; we are accountable before Him. Our moral failures carry consequences.

That's our basic problem. And if we can't see the problem, if we don't understand our fall from grace, we won't be able to understand and reach out for the solution. If we don't see the day of judgment rushing up to meet us, we won't pull the rip cord. And the "everlasting gospel," that essential parachute, can't save us. So God flies down through the heavens, in the person of these three angels, and shouts final instructions in our ear.

Now, let's look at what the first angel has to say. Revelation 14:7. The angel proclaims in a loud voice:

> Fear God and give glory to Him, for the hour of His judgment has come; and worship Him who made heaven and earth, the sea and springs of water (Revelation 14:7).

Let's examine this message carefully. The angel says, "Fear God and give glory to Him." Now, fearing God—that is, treating Him with awe and reverence—seems like a perfectly obvious thing to do. Why would God's final altar call begin this way? What danger is He trying to warn us about?

Well, one big problem is that our picture of God has been shrinking for some time. We rarely hear of a sovereign Lord outside time and space, whose reach stretches from horizon to horizon. These days, we almost always hear about God in terms of the personal Being who dwells in our hearts.

Of course, it's certainly true that God's Spirit can fill our hearts, but He isn't confined there. He isn't a pocket-sized God that we can carry around and send out on errands. There is much more to Him than just meeting our personal needs.But that is the picture of God that dominates today. The pocket-sized God is everywhere—proclaimed from pulpits, shared in Christian support groups, affirmed in self-help books. The pocket-sized God doesn't make any demands; He just helps us do whatever we want to do.

Our picture of God has been shrinking. What was once a vast canvas, is now just a pocket-size, passport photo. And that is why people find it so easy these days to re-imagine God, to create whatever kind of little deity is most convenient. We are falling head-long toward the end of time, and our perspective is distorted. Our God is too small. We are like sky divers who look down on big semi-trucks and think they're little ants.

So what does the first angel flying down toward us shout? "Give God reverence. Give God glory." Why? "The hour of His judgment has come."

There is an urgency about this message. There is a sense of supreme significance about it. In it we hear the drumbeat of eternity. It declares the hour of God's judgment *is come*—not *will* come in the far distant future.

It calls men and women to accountability—to moral responsibility—and pleads with us to realize that we are responsible for what we do.

We need to worship Him who made heaven and earth; we need to worship the Creator. That is precisely what is missing from our picture of God today. He has become the pocket-sized Handy Man. We no longer see Him as the great, majestic Creator of the universe. And we certainly don't see Him as the One who will judge us. God's last altar call is meant to correct our perspective, a perspective that can prove fatal.

Think about it. Isn't God's judgment the last thing people want to hear about, or think about, today? It's fine to talk about the love of our heavenly Father. It's fine to talk about God's acceptance. These things are true, and we want to hear them. That is what the pocket-sized God is good at—loving us and accepting us.

But God's judgment? That sounds so harsh; it is so condemning. Nobody wants to talk about that.

But God wants to talk about it. He is shouting it as His final warning. Why? For this reason: if there is no judgment, there is no gospel. Without God as the Creator and the Judge, you don't have a Saviour. Remember that the "everlasting gospel" is this first angel's primary message. The everlasting gospel is our parachute. That's how we survive an impact with the end time. But we've tangled up our rip cord, and we don't realize that our picture of God is causing the problem.

14 GOD'S LAST ALTAR CALL

Let me explain. Here is why reverencing God as Creator and as Judge is so important in preserving a hold on the "everlasting gospel." Let's start with how we lost our picture of God as Creator.

In 1831, a British ship, "The Beagle," began to sail down the western coast of South America. On board was a naturalist, Charles Darwin, whose observations would change the way most people look at the world. Today, Darwin's theory of evolution has become scientific orthodoxy. People see life as a struggle to survive; we have to make it up as we go along. Our purpose is not set for us by a superior Being. If we have a God, He is a pocket-sized God, One who goes with the flow, One who is part of the evolutionary process.

And guess what? When our picture of God as Creator gets smudged, our picture of God as Judge begins to fade too. In fact, the idea of any kind of moral judgment starts slipping away.

If we are just a product of the blind forces of nature, then how can we be held responsible for our actions? If we are involved in a process in which only the fittest survive, why not just try to survive—at any cost? And how can God judge human beings if everything about us, including our beliefs and our attitudes, is just nature taking its course?

This is the worldview that has been molding people's minds for over a century. This is what a secular age leaves us with—a pocket-sized God. He doesn't stand apart as Lord over all; He fits into human boundaries. He doesn't judge those who fight against His plan for mankind; He fits into *our* plans.

Lin Yutang was a third-generation Chinese Christian. His father served as a Presbyterian minister in a small village. But after Lin went through college and began teaching in Peking, he began to absorb the humanist ideas around him. Other forces conspired to shrink his picture of God as well. He bought into the Confucian concept of self-perfectibility through education. Humanity's potential grew larger and larger in his thinking; God grew smaller and smaller. Finally, the gospel just didn't make sense to Lin anymore. He couldn't accept the idea of a holy God having to redeem poor, wretched sinners.

Lin went on to make quite a name for himself as a scholar and bestselling author. Then one day, his Christian wife invited him to go to church with her. They were in New York City at the time. Lin wasn't much interested, but his belief that people could pull themselves up by their own bootstraps had begun to fray around the edges. It had become all too clear to Lin that, despite mankind's technological progress, men and women could still behave like savages in the twentieth century.

So Lin tagged along with his wife, and they attended a church on Madison Avenue. The minister was quite eloquent in his sermon on eternal life. But the topic didn't much interest Lin. The Christian heaven, with its pearly gates, didn't attract him. He dismissed it as appealing only to people who could never step inside Tiffany's, but hoped to do so in the next life.

Yet something he heard that day stuck in his head. "Could there really be something more to life than this secular routine?" The question haunted him and finally compelled him to take a closer look at the Bible. He told himself he was just re-reading the Gospels. But soon he found himself staring at God face to face—in the person of Christ. He discovered, as he later said, "the awe-inspiring simplicity and beauty of the teachings of Jesus. No one ever spoke like Jesus."

Lin's picture of God began to change. It grew bigger and bigger. He was astounded that God, as Jesus revealed Him, was so different from what people had made Him out to be.

Lin had started his search with this question: "Is there more to life than the secular; can there be a satisfying religion for the modern, educated man?" He ended his search sitting at Jesus' feet.

And now, the gospel made all the sense in the world to Lin. Now, it was materialism that didn't square with reality. He couldn't believe that the world was, as he said, "only a whirl of blind atoms obeying blind mechanical laws." No, human beings had real moral choices to make. Complacent, frail human beings had to accept or reject the gospel.

Lin Yutang found in Christ and His gospel, a complete sufficiency. He put it very simply, "Looking back on my life, I know that for thirty years I lived in this world like an orphan. I am an orphan no longer."

This remarkable man found a home in the gospel because his God was big enough. He had to change his perspective. He had to see the God who speaks absolute truth in love, the God who calls all men to account for their actions. And when he did so, Lin found himself a needy human being before this gracious God.

Do you see now why God sent this first angel flying down with this particular warning? Why the angel announced: "Fear God and give Him glory. The hour of His judgment is here. Worship the Creator"?

We need an alternative to our pocket-sized God. We need this particular picture of God that the first angel gives us. We need this particular perspective. Because reverencing God as Creator and as Judge will enable us to receive Christ as Saviour. It will help us be ready to pull the rip cord.

Christ is the one-and-only Saviour. Paul declares that believers are "justified freely by His [God's] grace through the redemption that is in Christ Jesus" (Romans 3:24).

Redemption, salvation, rescue—it's all in Christ Jesus.

THE POCKET-SIZED GOD 17

It's found nowhere else. So we need to accept Christ as our personal Saviour and acknowledge Him as Saviour each day.

We also need to acknowledge Christ as Lord. Read Paul's vivid picture in Philippians:

> Therefore God also has highly exalted Him [Christ] and given Him the name which is above every name, that at the name of Jesus every knee should bow, of those in heaven, and of those on earth, and of those under the earth, and that every tongue should confess that Jesus Christ is Lord (Philippians 2:9-11).

This isn't a pocket-sized God. This is the Lord of the universe. And we can only grasp His greatness on our knees, confessing His Lordship.

We must also acknowledge Christ as righteous Judge. Paul speaks of "the day when God will judge the secrets of men by Jesus Christ, according to my gospel" (Romans 2:16).

Jesus Christ is the God who sees into our innermost hearts. If we remain open to Him as our Saviour and Lord, then we will never have to fear Him as Judge. In fact, He will stand as our advocate in the judgment. But, if we try to hide from this God, if we keep secrets from Him, then those secrets will confront us in the day of judgment.

The day *is* coming when God will have to declare: "He who is unjust, let him be unjust still . . . he who is righteous, let him be righteous still" (Revelation 22:11). Our eternal destiny will be decided.

So please don't mistake Jesus Christ for a pocket-sized God you can manipulate. Acknowledge Jesus as Saviour. Acknowledge Jesus as Lord. Acknowledge Jesus as righteous Judge.

That is the only way we will avoid a fatal impact. There aren't a variety of parachutes around. There is just one—the everlasting gospel of Jesus Christ. It is the same gospel that rescued Paul in the first century. And it is the one that can rescue us in the end time.

Let's make sure that we have a firm hold on the true gospel. Let's make sure that we have a firm hold on the real God, the One who is Lord of the Universe, the One whose reach spreads from horizon to horizon.

A Tale of Two Churches

Sandy's friends craned their necks up at the blue sky and caught her tiny figure hurling itself out of the plane. This was her first time to jump without a line; Sandy was going to pull the rip cord herself.

Her friends far below, counted with her—one one thousand, two one thousand, three one thousand. But the parachute didn't open; nothing was happening. They waited as Sandy fell farther and farther. Why didn't she pull the rip cord? If something was wrong, what about her reserve chute?

Tragically, this young woman plummeted all the way to ground zero—and died instantly. When the ground crew rushed to the site, they noticed her parachute still folded neatly in the pack on her back. What had happened?

Then they saw the cloth of her jumpsuit torn away on the right side of her chest. It seemed as if she'd been desperately clawing at it. In fact, she'd dug through her clothing and actually lacerated her flesh with her fingers. The terrible truth dawned on them. Her rip cord was on her *left* side! In a moment of panic she had forgotten and kept pulling and yanking and clawing at the rip cord on the right that wasn't there.

I believe this tragedy reminds us that we are all plummeting toward an impact with the last days of earth's history. The end of earth is rushing up to meet us, and God wants to make sure that we open our parachutes—the everlasting gospel.

In the few chapters of this little book, we are studying God's final appeal to us in the end time—the message that three symbolic angels give us in Revelation 14. In the last chapter, we looked at the first angel's message. We read how the "everlasting gospel" is the foundation on which all three angels' messages are built. And in that chapter we saw how important it is to have the right perspective in order to really grasp that gospel. How important it is to acknowledge a sovereign Creator, Judge, and Saviour as we rush toward the time of the end.

In this chapter we are going to examine the second angel's message. We are going to see how this message relates to trying to grab a rip cord that isn't there, to grabbing hold of the wrong thing.

So let's take a look the message of the second angel that John saw flying in the midst of heaven. Here is what John wrote: "Another angel followed, saying, 'Babylon is fallen, is fallen, that great city, because she has made all nations drink of the wine of the wrath of her fornication' " (Revelation 14:8).

This may seem to be a rather odd warning at first. The fact that the city of Babylon has fallen is not exactly news. Babylon's fall and destruction was ancient history even when John wrote these words in the first century A.D. But, of course, Revelation is a book filled with symbols. Babylon and its fall stand for something—something we need to be aware of in the end time. Fortunately, the book of Revelation itself suggests what that is. In Revelation 17, Babylon is pictured as a woman dressed in purple and scarlet, decked out in gold and pearls. She is called the "Mother of Harlots" (verse 5). She is described as drunk with the blood of the saints (see verse 6).

Whom does this woman represent? Who is Babylon?

A TALE OF TWO CHURCHES   21

Here is the first clue. In many places in the Bible, when God's people fall into apostasy, they are pictured as unfaithful wives, promiscuous women. God takes it very personally when we turn to a false religion. Here is one typical example. In Jeremiah, a heartbroken Lord says: "Have you seen what backsliding Israel has done? She has gone up on every high mountain and under every green tree, and there played the harlot" (Jeremiah 3:6). What was Israel doing on those high mountains and under those green trees? Worshiping other gods. In the Lord's eyes, this was like becoming a harlot.

So, now in Revelation, we have a "scarlet woman" who is the "mother of all harlots." She must represent the source of false religion, a powerful conglomerate of apostate religion, both Christian and non-Christian.

Let's look at another clue. We can zero in on the identity of this scarlet woman, called Babylon, partly because of "the other woman," another symbolic woman found in the book of Revelation. Revelation is full of contrasts—the worship of the Lamb versus the worship of the beast; the glory of God versus the power of the dragon; the Holy City versus the lake of fire. Likewise, this scarlet woman stands in opposition to a very different woman described in chapter 12: "A great sign appeared in heaven: a woman clothed with the sun, with the moon under her feet, and on her head a garland of twelve stars" (verse 1).

The rest of this chapter makes it pretty clear who this woman is. She gives birth to a male child who is Jesus. She goes through a time of great persecution. This pure woman represents the pure church of Christ. In the New Testament the church is referred to as Christ's pure bride (see 2 Corinthians 11:2). So, here in Revelation, we see God's true church represented as a woman clothed with the sun.

Now, the scarlet woman, called Babylon, is her opposite number. The two figures stand in stark contrast. So, again, we can easily conclude that the scarlet woman must represent a false church, a false religious system.

The book of Revelation is, in part, a tale of two women—two churches or religious systems. It is the story of God's true church and an apostate church. This is a picture of the end time the book of Revelation lays out for us.

Let's return to the second angel's message and try to fit that warning into the picture.

What did the second angel say? "Babylon is fallen. She made all nations drink . . . of her fornication" (Revelation 14:8). Remember, promiscuity and fornication are symbols of apostasy. So this scarlet woman, this false church, spreads her false doctrine to "all nations."

In the end time, we're going to be facing a worldwide religious power that spreads false teaching. What are we to do? The logical response is spelled out in Revelation 18. Here we hear the second angel's message expanded: "Babylon the great is fallen, is fallen . . . Come out of her, my people, lest you share in her sins" (Revelation 18:2, 4).

If Babylon is fallen, then we had better get out fast! As we rush headlong toward an impact with the final days, we don't want to be caught inside a false religion that collapses around our ears. We don't want to get tangled up in Babylon's immorality and false teaching that will lead to rebellion against God's commandments and the principles of salvation.

Here's the basic picture. We have a pure woman, clothed with the sun; this represents God's true church. We have Babylon, the scarlet woman, the mother of harlots, representing an apostate religious system. And God sends down an angel to give us an urgent warning. What does this angel say? "Babylon is fallen. Get out!" The implication is not only that we ought to get *out of* a false religious system, but that we ought also to get *into* God's true church.

This is the message of the second angel. How do we apply it? What should we do? Let's focus on two important questions:

1. What are the characteristics of Babylon?
2. What does it mean to get out of Babylon?

I believe God is trying to focus our attention on the essence of true, healthy religion in comparison with the essence of false, unhealthy religion. He's trying to help us know exactly what to hold fast to as the end time approaches. There are some specific things about this "tale of two women" in Revelation that can help us do exactly that. Let's look at how these women are described and the picture will become even more clear.

First, look at how the pure woman of Revelation 12 makes her appearance. John introduces her in this way: "A great sign appeared in heaven: a woman clothed with the sun" (Revelation 12:1). This pure woman, God's true church, appears in heaven. That is, she has her origin in heaven. She is a great sign, something God produces, something supernatural from Him.

Now, let's look at how the "scarlet woman" makes her appearance. John finds her in "the wilderness," (Revelation 17:3). She comes out of the desert, riding on a scarlet beast. The scarlet woman, the false church, has its origin on earth. It is propelled forward by the beast. Revelation 17 also tells us this beast receives power and authority from the kings of the earth (see verse 13). In other words, it wields great political power. This false religious system advances on the basis of political, coercive power.

So here are the first elements of the picture. God's true church comes down from heaven. The false religious system arises from the earth. What we're talking about here is divine origin versus human origin—two different systems of religion, one man-made, the other given to us directly by God.

These two women also suggest two very different kinds of power. The pure woman is a great sign from God. She wields spiritual power, the power to move hearts and minds. The scarlet woman wields political power. Remember that she is described as drunk with the blood of the saints. The false church is quite capable of persecuting Christ's true followers.

Now, let's look at other contrasts between the two.

The pure woman is clothed with the sun. Throughout the New Testament we hear about the light of the gospel, the light of God's truth. And remember that the message of these three angels is given in the context of the "everlasting gospel." The everlasting gospel accompanies the very first angel. God's message for the last generation is Jesus Christ. Jesus' grace saves us; His power transforms us; He does for us what we cannot do for ourselves. This is called salvation by faith in Christ alone.

The scarlet woman, however, is clothed in purple and scarlet and holds a golden cup full of abominations. This false religious system may be seductively rich and appear prosperous, but it dispenses a corrupted form of the gospel in which human ideas and traditions overshadow the truths of God's Word. This false gospel always revolves around human efforts to work out our own security and salvation. And she makes all nations drunk with this distorted gospel. Please remember that every false religious system is based in some way on salvation by works, by human efforts.

Finally, the pure woman wears on her head a garland of twelve stars. Most commentators believe this represents the twelve apostles. In other words, her authority comes from the testimony of the apostles, from Scripture.

The scarlet woman, however, is covered with "names of blasphemy" (Revelation 17:3). The dictionary defines *blasphemy* in theological terms as the act of claiming for oneself the attributes and rights of God. "Names of blasphemy," then, refer to the titles this apostate system claims for itself which really belong only to God. So we have the last contrast between these two churches: God's true church takes its authority from the Word of God. The false system tries to make God's authority its own.

Here is what we have found so far:

> Pure Woman = God's true church
> 1. Divine origin
> 2. Spiritual power
> 3. Light of the gospel
> 4. Authority based on Word of God
>
> Scarlet woman = A false religious system
> 1. Human origin
> 2. Political, persecuting power
> 3. Seductive, distorted gospel
> 4. Usurps God's authority

May I suggest that these contrasts between the two women—between Babylon, the false church and Christ's true church—really boil down to a single thing: a man-made religion on the one hand, and on the other, a religion that comes from God. That is illustrated clearly when we think about the origin of ancient Babylon. Does the Tower of Babel ring a bell? That's where Babylon began.

You remember the story. The survivors of the flood wanted to build a tower tall enough to challenge the sovereignty of God. Instead of trusting in God's promise not to send another world-wide deluge, they decided to rely on the work of their own hands. They would build their own religious security system.

And you know, that same spirit of Babel persisted all through the centuries right up to the time of Babylon's great monarch, Nebuchadnezzar. He's the one who boasted, "Is not this great Babylon, that I have built for a royal dwelling by my mighty power and for the honor of my majesty?" (Daniel 4:30).

Babylon, the scarlet woman, represents man-made power, man-made teaching, man-made religion. It's the ultimate human do-it-yourself project. And the pure woman represents a religion that is from God, by God, and for God alone.

So here we have it. This is what the second angel's message is trying to make us aware of as we rush headlong into the end time. "Babylon is fallen! Come out of Babylon!" In other words, everything of merely human origin grows corrupt; everything man-made is going to fall apart in the end. We have to make sure we're clinging to the right way of salvation, the one way that comes straight from God.

Revelation defines, rather precisely, those who follow that right way. It describes faithful believers in the end time as those who "keep the commandments of God and have the testimony of Jesus Christ" (Revelation 12:17). You see, not all religions that lift up the right symbols are built on the testimony of Jesus, on the "everlasting gospel." Not all religions that use the right words about God are built on the authority of His Word, on His commandments. Sometimes the authority of human tradition takes the place of the Bible. Sometimes the political power that a church manages to wield can lead it away from the power of the gospel.

May I give you a few specific examples? Looking over the religious landscape today, I believe we can pick out a few present contrasts between a healthy religion that comes from God, and an unhealthy religion that is predominantly man-made. We can begin to see something about what God is warning us against.

Beware of any church or religion that shrinks the gospel of Jesus Christ, the gospel that declares sinful human beings are made right with God through what Christ accomplished on the cross. Some churches are turning away from the full New Testament picture of what salvation means and choosing a sliver of the gospel instead. Some just want the part about grace, not the part about law and judgment. They say, "God accepts everybody; He's not putting us down because of our sins." There is truth in this, of course. But it's only a sliver of the gospel, not the full picture.

Beware of those who reduce the gospel to feel-good psychology: "You're OK! Don't worry! Be happy!" This is a man-made reduction of the "everlasting gospel."

Beware of those who tend to bury the gospel under layers of church tradition. They may bury it under ritual, bury it under this or that theological system, bury it under plain old legalism, but the pure light of the gospel is dimmed by any man-made interpretations whatever they may be.

Healthy religion always involves discovering truth directly from the Bible and letting God speak His Word directly to our hearts. We have to bow humbly before the gospel of Jesus Christ and not try to compress it into some convenient box.

Always remember the picture of the true church given in Revelation 12—a woman appearing as a great sign in the heavens, clothed with the light of the sun. Spiritual light is always something that comes down to us from God. It's not something that we make up ourselves.

Do you know why this is so important today? Because, as we rush headlong toward the end of time, we want to make sure that we hang onto the right thing. We've got to cling to the real gospel, the means of rescue that God Himself created.

God wants to make sure that our parachute opens in time. He wants to make sure that we have a firm hold on the gospel. That is why he has given us this urgent warning: "Babylon is fallen! Come out of Babylon!" To come out of Babylon means to abandon all human substitutes for the gospel.

Will you make a commitment with me right now? Will you determine that you will base your life and your faith on what God reveals from His Word? Will you determine to judge all human ideas by the gospel of Jesus Christ instead of judging the gospel by human ideas?

Will you commit yourself to God's true church, to a body of believers who "keep the commandments of God and have the testimony of Jesus Christ" (Revelation 12:17)? Will you come into the safety of the everlasting gospel?

When Shepherds Turn Into Beasts

When Pastor Freeman spoke, the 2,000 people at Faith Assembly Church listened carefully, took notes, and nodded in agreement. His sermons lasted an hour, sometimes two. But the congregation hung on his every word and took his messages as authority for their lives.

Pastor Freeman had the right credentials. He had been a professor at Grace Theological Seminary in Indiana. He seemed so dedicated. He was regarded as "the genius behind Faith Assembly." There was a sense that he could never be replaced there. And yet this pastor led his congregation into a terrible tragedy. It's estimated that some eighty people, many of them children, died as a result of following his teachings.

Pastor Freeman didn't lead anyone off into the jungle to commit suicide. He didn't arm his parishioners in some compound and then set it ablaze. No, he simply insisted it was a sin to go to a doctor. He taught that all medicine is evil and satanic and that every illness or injury can be cured by a positive confession of faith. Members of the Faith Assembly sect followed this teaching to the letter. No doctor visits. No pre-natal care. They refused immunizations and took seat belts from their cars.

When church members died, it was assumed they didn't

have enough faith. The death toll increased. Faith Assembly women were a hundred times more likely to die giving birth than were women in the general population. And their babies were three times more likely to die.

Finally, Pastor Freeman and other church members were indicted on charges of aiding and inducing reckless homicide. When the news broke, people wondered how such a situation could possibly take place in a Christian church? How could apparently sincere Christian believers follow a man so blindly?

That question will become increasingly important in the end time of earth's history. How can we be sure who it really is that we are following? How can we be sure we are clinging to the "everlasting gospel" and not to some distortion of the gospel?

The question of whom we follow is addressed in very graphic terms by the third angel of Revelation 14. The three angels, who appear here in Revelation, give God's final warning, His last altar call, as the world rushes toward a rendezvous with Christ's second coming.

Earlier in this book, we've described the first angel flying in the midst of heaven as he gives his urgent message to earth. We've looked at the second angel swooping down with an announcement for all mankind as he likewise proclaims his message in a loud voice. Now, we turn our attention to the final messenger, the third angel. His warning from God, given as planet Earth hurtles toward the end time, is the most urgent and the most shocking of all.

Here is how the apostle John describes the last in this series of crucial messages in Revelation 14:

> Then a third angel followed them, saying with a loud voice, "If anyone worships the beast and his image, and receives his mark on his forehead or on his hand, he himself shall also drink

WHEN SHEPHERDS TURN INTO BEASTS 31

of the wine of the wrath of God" (Revelation 14:9, 10).

Here we have a warning about worshiping the beast. And the language of this warning is extremely vivid; it's almost shocking, in fact. The angel goes on to picture fire and brimstone, torment, and smoke rising forever and ever. It's a fearful picture, one of the most urgent warnings in the whole Bible. And it relates to worshiping the beast.

Obviously, worship of the beast poses a great danger in the end time. God is shouting in our ear. He is telling us what to beware of as we hurtle toward impact with the end time. But please remember that God is shouting to us because of His great Father love. He's like a parent who sees his child wander out into a busy street. He shouts so urgently because he wants to rescue us so much.

So, what is this matter of worshiping "the beast" all about? What does it mean? A warning—a danger sign—isn't much good unless we understand it.

Let's start by looking at what worshiping the beast is *not*. Remember that Revelation is a book full of contrasts, full of opposites. Worshiping the beast in Revelation stands in stark contrast to worshiping the Lamb. This book gives us vivid scenes of multitudes worshiping the Lamb of God. They proclaim, "Worthy is the Lamb who was slain to receive power . . . and honor and glory" (Revelation 5:12).

The Lamb is Jesus Christ. God's faithful people are said to "follow the Lamb wherever He goes" (Revelation 14:4). They are unconditionally loyal to Christ and His everlasting gospel.

In contrast to this holy and healthy worship, Revelation paints a very different picture: "All the world marveled and followed the beast . . . they worshiped the beast, saying, 'Who is like the beast? Who is able to make war with him?' And he was given a mouth speaking great things and blasphemies, and he was given authority" (Revelation 13:3-5).

This chapter warns us that everyone on earth whose name is not written in the Lamb's Book of Life at the end time, will be worshiping the beast. In other words, we're either going to be worshiping the Lamb or the beast—one or the other. No one will remain on the sidelines. There won't be any neutral corners. It is the climax of the great struggle between Christ and Satan that has been going on for thousands of years, and every human being will stand on one side or the other.

But why will so many people follow and worship this evil antichrist power, this beast?

The passage itself suggests an answer. The beast speaks great things. People marvel at what he says: "Who is like the beast?" (verse 4). He has great authority; he has great influence and power. He will seem like great *spiritual* power.

Later in Revelation 13, we learn that the beast deceives people, in part, because he performs great signs. He can even make fire come down from heaven (see verse 13). In other words, the beast doesn't *look* like some terrible, evil figure. What this passage really describes is a seductive, charismatic, powerful, authoritative religious leader. He is a shepherd! He may even quote from the Bible and use Christian language. But he is a shepherd who becomes a beast!

Why will so many people follow and worship this end-time figure? Because they want someone who is powerful to lead them. They want someone who speaks great things, someone who speaks with authority. The man who shouts that all truth has been revealed to him always attracts a crowd. The man who performs great signs always attracts a crowd.

Let me give you a few examples that demonstrate ex-

WHEN SHEPHERDS TURN INTO BEASTS 33

actly how shepherds turn into beasts. We need to be able to spot the danger signs.

In 1985, an epidemic of divorce broke out among the members of Seattle's Community Chapel. In one year, some two dozen couples divorced or began divorce proceedings. The reason wasn't hard to find.

Church members had begun practicing what were called "spiritual connections." Men and women, usually not spouses, were supposed to experience a deeper level of Christian love with one another. And they made these "connections" by spending a lot of time together and by dancing together in the church. Expressions of affection with someone else's spouse understandably led to the breakup of many homes.

Reading about a tragedy such as this, we wonder: How could something so bizarre happen in a Christian church?

It happened because these people followed Pastor Donald Barnett. They followed him devotedly and unquestioningly. Barnett claimed to have experienced a heavenly vision. He said, "The Lord promised to give me truth that He has not given to man before." It was after he had a mystical encounter with a dancing angel that Barnett introduced his church members to the practice of intimate dancing between men and women who were not married to each other.

This is the first sign of danger we need to be aware of. This is how shepherds turn into beasts. They always claim to have a corner on the truth. They claim that God has revealed the whole picture to them and to no one else. David Barnett warned his church members against the indiscriminate use of a wide variety of Christian books and magazines. He wanted them to listen to his own tapes. He told them *he alone* needed to decide questions of doctrine.

One former member put it very clearly, "People at Community Chapel, thinking that they are placing their allegiance in the Word of God, are actually placing their allegiance in a man and his interpretation of the Word of God." (*Christianity Today,* August 8, 1986, 33).

Paul wrote to believers in Thessalonica about conditions at the end of time. He warned them: "That Day will not come unless the falling away comes first, and the man of sin is revealed, . . . who opposes and exalts himself above all that is called God" (2 Thessalonians 2:3, 4).

Why do people fall away from the faith? Because they follow someone who exalts himself above God. He may say wonderful things about God, but the bottom line is that it's *his* interpretation of the truth that counts in the end. He is the final authority.

Beware of charismatic religious leaders who claim that they alone know the truth, that they alone are listening to God. The call of that shepherd will soon turn into the roar of a beast.

The second danger sign is closely related to the first. David Koresh is a good example. He somehow persuaded his Branch Davidian followers that, since he had a special connection with King David, he could have several wives. He could have sexual relations with various women in the church. He also persuaded members that preparing for the end time involved stockpiling assault rifles and hand grenades. The result was the tragic, fiery disaster at Waco.

Shepherds who turn into beasts always make up their own rules. It's not enough for them to follow the basic teachings of the Bible. They have to promote and enforce their own revised version of the truth.

Pastor Donald Barnett couldn't just encourage Christian fellowship. He had to promote private dancing sessions for those who wanted a new level of spiritual experience.

WHEN SHEPHERDS TURN INTO BEASTS

Pastor Hobart Freeman couldn't just encourage the afflicted to have faith in God. He had to tell them it was a sin to go to a doctor.

Shepherds who turn into beasts always make up their own rules; they always go beyond the clear teachings of Scripture which are available to everyone. They want to speak with great authority about great things that no one else knows about. They often use their "special revelations" to control their followers, sometimes trying to regulate every detail of their lives.

Paul explains exactly why people are victimized by such leaders. He gives this warning: "The coming of the lawless one is according to the working of Satan . . . with all unrighteous deception among those who perish, because they did not receive the love of the truth, that they might be saved" (2 Thessalonians 2:9,10).

What determines whether you will be deceived by "the lawless one," by a false religious leader? It boils down to this: a love of the truth. If you allow God to build in you a love for His truth, the truth of Scripture, then you'll be safe. But if you are willing to close your eyes to difficult truths and accept easier, seductive lies, then you'll be vulnerable.

We must nourish a love of God's truth. And remember that in the Bible, truth is a Person, the person of Jesus Christ, the One who said "I am the way, the truth, and the life" (John 14:6). We must keep our eyes fixed on this glorious Saviour and turn away from shepherds who turn into beasts. That is the warning the third angel gives us. He gives it in such graphic language because sincere believers can be destroyed by shepherds who turn into beasts.

The angel warns us about worshiping the beast, but he also warns us about something else—he warns us against receiving the mark of the beast. Revelation chapter 13, tells us that in the end time the beast:

> causes all . . . to receive a mark on their right hand or on their foreheads, and that no one may buy or sell except one who has the mark or the name of the beast, or the number of his name" (Revelation 13:16, 17).

Christians have endlessly speculated about what the mark of the beast is and exactly how it is enforced. At one time, those computer labels that the grocery store clerk scans at the check-out counter, were suspect. Others wondered about our ID numbers at the bank or about that hand stamp they use at some amusement parks for reentry. But the mechanics of the mark of the beast aren't that important. The whole world today is interconnected through computers. People can be traced and identified in any number of ways.

The important thing is what this mark *means*. Obviously, it is a sign of allegiance to the beast—something internal, not just external. It's a mark of loyalty to the beast as opposed to loyalty to the Lamb of God. It's something the exact opposite of the everlasting gospel. Every false religious system is based on salvation by works; every false religious system distorts the beautiful gospel of salvation by faith in Jesus Christ alone.

Remember the characteristic danger signs of shepherds who turn into beasts? They claim that they alone know the truth, that they alone can interpret Scripture. And they make up their own rules beyond what God has revealed in the Bible.

So, if the mark of the beast is a sign of allegiance to the beast, it must represent allegiance to the beast's version of the truth. It must be a sign that shows you are following the beast's teachings and not the teachings of the Bible.

Let me give you an illustration of how this can happen—even inside the Christian church.

WHEN SHEPHERDS TURN INTO BEASTS 37

When the Roman emperor, Constantine, publicly accepted the Christian faith in AD 312, it spelled a new day for the church. Just a few years before, believers had been thrown to the lions in Rome and hunted down like wild animals in North Africa. But now, Christianity was accepted; soon it would become the official religion of the Roman Empire.

Now, all kinds of pagans who had been worshiping Zeus or Caesar wanted to join the Christian church. Unfortunately, many church leaders decided to make the transition easier by allowing these new members to hang on to some pagan ideas, images, and customs. Sun worship had a very strong hold on the people of the Roman Empire. And it didn't exactly wither away when pagans began calling on the name of Jesus.

So, the Emperor Constantine thought of a way to make sun-worshipers feel more at home in the Christian church. In March, AD 321, he issued this decree: "On the venerable Day of the Sun let the magistrates and people residing in cities rest, and let all work shops be closed."

This was the first step toward establishing Sunday as the official day of rest and worship for Christians. Soon the church itself would forbid all work on Sunday.

What most people don't realize today, is that the seventh day, Saturday, remained the Christian day of worship for some time after Christ's death. That was the Sabbath for early believers. There is certainly no evidence for the change of the day of worship in the New Testament. But finally, Christian church leaders decided to accommodate sun-worship. After all, they said, Sunday was also the day of the Lord's resurrection.

Now, why is this important? Does it really matter what day of the week we go to church on? Isn't God happy when we worship Him, no matter what day it is? Of course He is.

The important thing was what people were saying in their hearts when they began to worship on Sunday, what this new sign of allegiance meant to them. That is what God cares about. Were they really worshiping Jesus Christ, the resurrected Lord? Or were they really still worshiping the sun?

As we look at the history of the church, it's obvious that quite a number of its members were still worshiping someone or something besides Jesus. In the middle of the fifth century, we find Pope Leo I rebuking worshipers at St. Peter's Cathedral, because they kept turning around and bowing toward the sun before entering the basilica.

This mixing of pagan customs with Christian teaching greatly weakened the church. And I believe that Sunday worship had something to do with the tragedy.

This rather arbitrary change in the day of worship from the seventh day of the week to the first also contributed to another problem—the problem of church authority. The Christian church kept increasing in power and in authority right into the Middle Ages. It became the official interpreter of Scripture, and eventually it began to persecute those who questioned its authority.

When individuals challenged the church on these points, church leaders sometimes used a very interesting argument to defend their right to determine what God's truth is. They pointed to the observance of Sunday. "We did that by our own authority," they said. "There is no basis for it in Scripture."

Do you see the danger of making up our own rules, our own signs? It can become a question of allegiance. Whom are we really following? Who has the last word?

Listen to Paul's admonition in Romans 6: "Don't you know that when you offer yourselves to someone to obey him as slaves, you are slaves to the one whom you obey—whether you are slaves to sin, which leads to death, or to

WHEN SHEPHERDS TURN INTO BEASTS

obedience, which leads to righteousness?" (Romans 6:16, NIV).

We are either going to give our ultimate allegiance to the Word of God or to some religious leader. If Scripture and Scripture alone doesn't have the last word, then we get into trouble very fast.

Hobart Freeman's congregation found that out—too late. Only after burying their babies because they refused to see a doctor, did his members begin to question his authority and their blind allegiance.

Donald Barnett's congregation found that out—too late. They didn't wake up until indiscriminate "intimate dancing" had broken families apart.

And I believe congregations during the time of Constantine found that out—too late. Before pastors of his day realized how many people were still worshiping the sun on the new "holy day," the church had been irreparably damaged. It was a question of allegiance. Sunday became, for them, a sign of the wrong allegiance, a mark of the wrong kind of worship.

Who has the last word, the authoritative word, in our lives? A shepherd who can turn into a beast? Or the Lamb of God? That is the question.

We can't just make up the rules ourselves. We can't let any leader, no matter how spiritually powerful and charismatic he may be, make up the rules for us. We have to give our allegiance totally and exclusively to Jesus Christ, the Lamb of God. He alone can keep us safe in His love and truth. What will count in the end is worshiping and following and listening to Him. And that is all that will count.

We are falling headlong toward an impact with the end times. God is eager to rescue each of us with His everlasting gospel. He doesn't want any shepherd who turns into a beast to get in the way of that rescue. That is why the warning these three angels give is so loud, so urgent. That's why God's last altar call of love is so vivid.

Can It Reach the Whole World?

There is a force set loose on this planet which is hurling us toward the end of the world. It's pushing us toward an impact with the end of time. It's powerful, more powerful than almost anyone realizes, and it has a supernatural source. Yet it remains hidden from most people's view.

What is this force?

No, it's not some New Age movement or conspiracy. No, it's not environmental disasters piling up on each other. No, it's not underground Satanism or secular humanism. None of those dark forces are capable of propelling us into the end time.

The force I'm talking about is simply this: the gospel going to all the world. Believe it or not, that is the most powerful force at work on our planet today.

If you really understand what is going on in the world today, you won't just see religious people trying to do their duty; you won't see business as usual. You will see a powerful movement of God that is building in momentum, enormous momentum, right now.

God is moving in a variety of ways through a variety of Christian groups around the world. I want to give you a glimpse of that force at work in the midst of just one Christian group—my own Seventh-day Adventist Church.

Did you know that the gospel going to all the world is the result of both a command and of a promise?

The command is recorded in Matthew 28. Just before Jesus ascended to heaven He gave His final command to His disciples: "Go therefore and make disciples of all the nations . . . teaching them to observe all things that I have commanded you" (Matthew 28:19, 20).

Here you have it! This is the great commission given to all followers of Christ. But it is also a promise. In Matthew 24, Jesus puts it this way: "And this gospel of the kingdom will be preached in all the world as a witness to all the nations, and then the end will come" (Matthew 24:14).

The gospel *will* be preached all over the world, and *then* the end will come. That promise is echoed at the beginning of the three angels' messages in the heart of the book of Revelation. The first angel messenger tells us, that the everlasting gospel will be preached "to those who dwell on the earth—to every nation, tribe, tongue and people" (Revelation 14:6).

Now, when we look at places like America and Europe, it's not too hard to believe that the gospel can indeed reach every person. There are plenty of Christian groups working hard to do just that.

But what about the remote corners of the earth? What about those isolated tribes and stone-age cultures? Can the gospel of Jesus Christ really reach every tribe, tongue, and people on the earth?

Well, let's go and see.

Let's go to Iryan Jaya, half an island that used to be called New Guinea. This is about as far from First Baptist Church on Main Street, USA as you can get. It's one of the most isolated regions of the earth. Many of the tribes living in these mountains in the interior have had contact with outsiders only in the last few decades.

CAN IT REACH THE WHOLE WORLD? 43

So, let's pay the tiny village of Bora Bora a visit. There are only about 300 people here. But guess what we find? A small Seventh-day Adventist Church. An Adventist Bible teacher has been quite busy sharing the gospel. And more than one hundred of the Bora Bora villagers have been baptized into Jesus Christ!

We fly off again and drop into the town of Arimes. What do we find? A baptism is going on, and an Adventist elder is praying for a sick child.

In the village of Asame, there was no Adventist congregation just a year ago. Now they have built a chapel and have filled it with a growing congregation, eager to continue sharing the faith. There are now some 150,000 Adventist believers on the island made up of Iryan Jaya and Papua New Guinea.

The gospel of Jesus Christ *is* going to the remotest corners of the earth. It's building in momentum, and it's doing so for only one reason—the power of God. The gospel is, after all, the power of God. It's not just some human strategy. It's not human skill. It's God's hand moving people's hearts—in every part of the earth.

Quite recently, a team of four Adventists made a trek through the rocky hills and rivers of the central Philippines. They entered a completely isolated area, inaccessible by motor vehicle. The people who live there are animists who worship the objects of nature.

After hiking through the jungle for eight hours, these Adventist Christians came to a village. And what did they find? A building already erected for the worship of God! It was there waiting for them!

A villager had dreamed of a man dressed in white linen with shining shoes who said, "Build a big house for God and worship Him." He also said some people would be arriving who would teach "Bible truth." Another villager dreamed of a man telling her that the coming visitors were good people.

So, these four Adventists began teaching about Jesus Christ and His gospel. The villagers were amazed, and they accepted the message warmly. Soon there were twenty-four baptized believers to fill that "big house for God."

Can God's hand reach into the most inaccessible places of the earth? You bet it can! Today, right now, we're seeing the fulfillment of Jesus' promise to the disciples: "You shall be witnesses to me . . . to the end of the earth" (Acts 1:8).

There is another reason why the gospel is gathering such tremendous momentum. Besides reaching into remote, primitive areas, the gospel is doing something else that is remarkable. It's breaking down barriers that have stood for half a century. The iron curtain that closed off the communist world from Christian witness for so long has been torn to shreds. And the gospel is rushing in to fill an enormous spiritual vacuum in the lives of millions.

Nothing quite this dramatic, nothing on this grand a scale, has happened in the history of Christian missions. The force of the gospel is bowling over barriers. Let me give you a couple of examples that you probably haven't heard very much about.

Albania was long known as the most rigid and repressive of all the communist states. The bunkers built through the land and the militant slogans proclaimed everywhere seemed to completely isolate the Albanian people from the rest of the world. It was difficult to fathom how the gospel could ever penetrate the country.

But now the gospel is spreading rapidly. I'm especially excited about it because while serving my church in Europe, I coordinated a plan to try to reach the Albanian people through radio. Now, my associate David Curry, has conducted an evangelistic series in the capital city, Korce, and a new church has been established with more than 150 believers worshiping there! The joy of the gospel is being multiplied.

CAN IT REACH THE WHOLE WORLD? 45

I'll never forget what a young woman said just after her baptism in Korce: "I was so happy, honestly I was too happy to cry. I saw the others crying, but I couldn't cry, really. I think that wherever I go and whatever I do, I will have Jesus in my life so He will live in me."

Mongolia is another area of the world that has been almost completely cut off from the gospel. The land is frozen much of the year. The people, traditionally, have been suspicious of outsiders. But that didn't stop a courageous young Adventist couple, Brad and Cathie Jolly. In October 1991, they began their work in the city of Ulan Bator, trying to break down barriers. They learned the language and adopted local customs. Brad and Cathie began meeting privately in their small apartment with groups of young people. They had to keep a very low profile, of course, in order not to arouse the suspicions of the authorities.

Two years later, their efforts culminated in one of the first Christian baptisms in Mongolia in many decades. It was a historic occasion, and Pastor Robert Folkenberg, General Conference President of the Seventh-day Adventist Church, officiated. About forty young people stood by as three individuals were lowered into the water and raised to the newness of life, sealing the commitment of their lives to Jesus Christ.

Pastor Folkenberg reported,

> I have to say this was one of the most moving baptisms I've ever been a part of.... When they gave their testimony, I couldn't understand all their words, of course, but I could see clearly how much that day meant to them.
>
> It's events like this one in Ulan Bator that give me a sense that the gospel of Jesus Christ is indeed breaking down barriers. It's racing over new ground and it's penetrating new people groups.

> As I travel all over the world, I can't help but be excited about the scope of God's great work—transforming human lives.

The gospel of Jesus Christ is reaching the remotest areas of the earth and breaking down barriers.

"But wait a minute," you may be thinking. "Let's be realistic. What about the problem of sheer numbers? There are billions of people on this planet. Can we really expect to reach all of them with the gospel—in one generation? Can we even keep up with population growth?"

Well, let's take a look!

Brazil is a good example of a country with a booming population. Millions are crowded into its major cities. Many of them are poor, many of them apparently unreached by the gospel. But let me tell you about what happened in the summer of 1993. Our sister organization, "The Voice Of Prophecy," conducted a series of evangelistic rallies throughout Brazil. It was the fiftieth anniversary of the radio broadcast in that country.

What happened?

What happened can be described only as God's Spirit moving on the masses. It wasn't just that people came and filled churches. People came and filled *stadiums!* Thirty thousand persons poured into a huge soccer stadium in Belem, for example. Another 30,000 filled the stands in the city of Salvador.

Lonnie Melashenko reported: "As a result of Brazil '93, one million people have enrolled in the Voice Of Prophecy Bible School courses—and some 20,000 baptisms have taken place. It's just overwhelming. It's thrilling to see just a little of what God is doing."

I understand Lonnie Melashenko's feelings very well. I can understand because of what happened during our "It Is Written" meetings at Moscow's Olympic Stadium. God

CAN IT REACH THE WHOLE WORLD? 47

magnified our efforts. He turned the meetings into a major event in the city. Thousands upon thousands attended. Participants in that city completed half a million Bible study lessons! I've never seen such an enormous hunger for the Word of God.

But there is another reason I'm very confident that the gospel can go to the entire world—even in the face of the world's growing population. I know what God has been doing through radio and television.

In January 1994, Adventist World Radio began a powerful broadcast from two 250-kilowatt transmitters in the new Republic of Slovakia. That station began regular twenty-four-hour-a-day broadcasts of Christian programming in Arabic, Czech, English, French, German, and in India's four major languages. This means Adventist World Radio is now covering all of central and eastern Africa, all of India, and all of the Middle East with the good news of Jesus Christ!

And then, there is the newly-built Adventist Media Center in Tula, Russia. Gospel radio programs are sent out from Tula in eight languages every day. These programs, which have introduced 65,000 people to Bible study, cover southern Europe, much of Asia, and extend into China. They are transmitted through five of the Russian government's most powerful facilities. Transmitters, which used to jam radio signals coming in from the West, are now used to proclaim the gospel of Jesus Christ! Adventist World Radio carries the radio version of the "It Is Written" program. It now covers three-quarters of the world's population!

Yes, the good news of the gospel is going out to the billions. God is also doing marvelous things through our "It Is Written" international telecast. Besides the programming that covers hundreds of cities here at home in North America, the translated program is shown in twenty-three major cities of the former Soviet Union. In Brazil, "It Is Written" has an estimated ten million viewers each week!

And now, our international ministry is taking another giant step forward. "It Is Written" has brought in Russian, Brazilian, and Spanish pastors to begin taping programs in their own languages. This ministry is truly becoming an international telecast. Now, along with my translated messages, millions of Russia's citizens can also see programs with Pastor Daniel Reband. Millions of Brazilians will be viewing programs by Pastor Alejandro Bullon. Soon, we plan to make additional programs by Pastor Milton Peverini in Spanish available to Spain and countries throughout Latin America. Several are already taped and ready to go!

The gospel truly is going out to all the world, in over 2,000 languages. The Word of God has become a great force touching the lives of millions today.

Yes, Jesus *is* coming again very soon. How do we know? Because the gospel of Christ is building in momentum. It's penetrating to the remotest corners of the earth. It's breaking down age-old barriers. And it's reaching entire countries—millions of people through the media.

The force that is impelling us straight for the end time is the force of the Spirit of God, spreading the good news.

God wants you to be part of His mighty movement as we approach the end time. He wants you to be carried along by the momentum of the gospel of Jesus Christ. Won't you determine right now in your own heart that you will be ready to meet Jesus when He comes? Won't you answer His last altar call? Won't you accept Jesus as your Saviour and give your life to Him? He's waiting for your decision. He's calling to you.